WHAT DO THEY DO?

WHAT DO FARMERS DO ALL DAY?

By Emily Mahoney

Gareth Stevens PUBLISHING

Please visit our website, www.garethstevens.com. For a free color catalog of all our high-quality books, call toll free 1-800-542-2595 or fax 1-877-542-2596.

Library of Congress Cataloging-in-Publication Data

Names: Mahoney, Emily Jankowski, author.
Title: What do farmers do all day? / Emily Mahoney.
Description: New York : Gareth Stevens Publishing, [2021] | Series: What do they do? | Includes index. | Contents: An important job—Caring for livestock—Farming crops—Making Money—Feeding the world.
Identifiers: LCCN 2019054813 | ISBN 9781538256893 (library binding) | ISBN 9781538256879 (paperback) | ISBN 9781538256886 (6 Pack) | ISBN 9781538256909 (ebook)
Subjects: LCSH: Farmers—Juvenile literature. | Agriculture—Juvenile literature.
Classification: LCC HD8039.F3 .M34 2020 | DDC 630.23—dc23
LC record available at https://lccn.loc.gov/2019054813

Published in 2021 by
Gareth Stevens Publishing
111 East 14th Street, Suite 349
New York, NY 10003

Copyright © 2021 Gareth Stevens Publishing

Editor: Emily Mahoney
Designer: Laura Bowen

Photo credits: Series art Dima Polies/Shutterstock.com; cover, p. 1 Monkey Business Images/Shutterstock.com; p. 5 Gallo Images-Stuart Fox/The Images Bank/Getty Images Plus/Getty Images; p. 7 Iakov Filimonov/Shutterstock.com; p. 9 Junko Takahashi/a.collectionRF/Getty Images; p. 11 JackF/iStock/Getty Images Plus/Getty Images; p. 13 Loop Images/Contributor/Universal Images Group Editorial/Getty Images; p. 15 Rick Dalton/Passage/Getty Images Plus/Getty Images; p. 17 Siegfried Layda/Photographer's Choice/Getty Images Plus/Getty Images; p. 19 VW Pics/Contributor/Universal Images Group Editorial/Getty Images; p. 21 RgStudio/E+/Getty Images.

All rights reserved. No part of this book may be reproduced in any form without permission in writing from the publisher, except by a reviewer.

Printed in the United States of America

Some of the images in this book illustrate individuals who are models. The depictions do not imply actual situations or events.

CPSIA compliance information: Batch #CS20GS: For further information contact Gareth Stevens, New York, New York, at 1-800-542-2595.

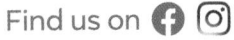

CONTENTS

An Important Job. 4

Caring for Livestock. 6

Farming Crops. 12

Making Money. 18

Feeding the World. 20

Glossary. 22

For More Information. 23

Index 24

Boldface words appear in the glossary.

An Important Job

You may not think about it much, but you can thank a farmer for most foods that you eat! From the meat for your cheeseburger to the carrot sticks in your lunch, much of the food we eat starts on a farm! Read on to find out what a farmer's day is like.

Caring for Livestock

Some farmers raise **livestock**, while other farmers raise **crops**. Some farmers do both! If a farmer has animals, their first job of the day is to feed the animals and give them fresh water. Farmers may then milk cows or goats, or collect eggs from chickens.

Caring for live animals is a lot of work. The animals need a clean place to sleep, so farmers may spend time cleaning, or mucking out, **stalls**. They have to fix up the barn where the animals live. Farmers may also need to order food for the animals or even give them a bath!

Farmers must make sure that their livestock stay healthy. They need to make sure that they **vaccinate** their animals. Farmers take their livestock to the veterinarian, or animal doctor, if they're sick. After all, farmers want their animals to make good milk, eggs, and wool to sell!

Farming Crops

If a farmer is responsible for crops, they must make sure that their crops are watered. They have to be sure there aren't any weeds in their fields. They also need to **fertilize** the fields to help their crops to grow. Depending on the time of year, they may also need to plant seeds.

Farmers use many machines to help them to do their job, such as tractors, balers, seeders, and plows. Combines are used to **harvest** crops. Once the farmer's morning jobs are done, they might spend some time **maintaining** or fixing these machines to make sure everything is working properly.

A farmer must also harvest the crops once they are ready to be picked. This can be done by hand or with machines. Once crops are harvested, they must be cleaned and packaged before they are able to leave the farm. Then, they are loaded onto trucks that take crops where they will be sold.

Making Money

Farms are businesses. Farmers spend time keeping track of money they've made. They find new ways to make money too. Some farmers may choose to sell their milk, eggs, or crops at a **farmers' market**. Other farmers may sell them at a store near you!

Feeding the World

A farmer's job is not only busy but also very important! Without farmers, we wouldn't have fresh fruits and vegetables, or healthy animals for meat and animal products. So, the next time you bite into a crisp apple, don't forget that a farmer helped that food reach your mouth!

GLOSSARY

crops: food that is grown to be sold

farmers' market: a place where goods, such as crops, milk, and eggs, are sold right from farmers to people who live nearby

fertilize: to add natural chemicals to soil to help plants grow

harvest: to gather crops from the field

livestock: farm animals, like cows, sheep, or pigs

maintain: to care for something by making repairs and changes when needed

stall: an area in a barn where an animal is kept

vaccinate: to give a person or animal a drug to keep them from getting an illness

FOR MORE INFORMATION

BOOKS

Brisson, Pat. *Before We Eat: From Farm to Table*. Thomaston, ME: Tilbury House Publishers, 2018.

Paul, Baptiste, and Miranda Paul. *I Am Farmer: Growing an Environmental Movement in Cameroon.* Minneapolis, MN: Millbrook Press, 2019.

WEBSITES

Farm Facts & Worksheets
kidskonnect.com/science/farms/
This website has great information and fun activities about farming.

Farming Facts for Kids
kids.kiddle.co/Farming
Find interesting information about farming in a kid-friendly format here.

Publisher's note to educators and parents: Our editors have carefully reviewed these websites to ensure that they are suitable for students. Many websites change frequently, however, and we cannot guarantee that a site's future contents will continue to meet our high standards of quality and educational value. Be advised that students should be closely supervised whenever they access the internet.

INDEX

balers 14

combines 14

crops 6, 12, 14, 16, 18

eggs 6, 10, 18

farmers' markets 18

feeding animals 6, 8

fertilizing crops 12

harvesting crops 14, 16

livestock/animals 6, 8, 10, 20

machines 14, 16

milk/milking 6, 10, 18

packaging crops 16

planting seeds 12

plows 14

seeders 14

stalls/barns 8

tractors 14

watering crops 12

wool 10